DATE DUE

DEMCO 38-297

A Discovery Biography

Abraham Lincoln

— ◆ —

For the People

by Anne Colver
illustrated by William Moyers

CHELSEA JUNIORS
A division of Chelsea House Publishers
New York ◆ Philadelphia

This book is for Grier and Ann Graff

The Discovery Biographies have been prepared under the educational supervision of Mary C. Austin, Ed.D., reading specialist and professor of education, Case Western Reserve University.

Cover illustration: John Paul Genzo

First Chelsea House edition 1992

1 3 5 7 9 8 6 4 2

ISBN   0-7910-1414-2

Contents

Abraham Lincoln:
For the People

Chapter *1*

Rolling Off a Log

"Let's go down to the creek and see if there are any fish," young Abraham Lincoln said to his visiting friend. "I wish we could go swimming. But we can't, because it's Sunday."

It was a hot Sunday afternoon in June. Young Abe was seven years old. His friend Austin Gollaher was eight. Austin's family had driven their horse and wagon over miles of rough Kentucky roads to visit Abe's family.

It was a treat for the Lincolns to have company. In 1816, Kentucky was pioneer country. Families lived in log cabins they built themselves. There were no neighbors nearby.

The two boys were restless, listening to the grownups talk and talk. They were glad to get away by themselves.

"We can go across the log bridge to the island," Abe said. "I saw some partridges there yesterday."

The boys started across. Knob Creek was flooded by heavy rains. The logs were slippery under their feet.

Splash! Young Abe fell in the water!

Neither of the boys knew how to swim. The water was so deep it was over Abe's head. And the current was fast.

Austin threw out a long stick. He held one end. Abe caught the other end. Abe gasped and spluttered. He nearly dragged his friend in. Finally Austin pulled Abe ashore.

"Thank goodness you didn't drown," Austin said. He pounded Abe on the back to help him get his breath.

The boys put their clothes on the rocks to dry. The sun stayed hot. Soon the boys could dress again. They pulled their trousers smooth and slicked down their hair.

Young Abe grinned. "Nobody would ever guess we had a swim," he said. His blue eyes twinkled.

Austin looked suspicious. Abe Lincoln was the smartest boy in school. He had learned to read faster than anyone.

Abe loved mischief. He was always thinking up new pranks. Once the teacher had said, "Abe Lincoln, you must have two imps inside of you. One good imp, and one bad imp."

"Abe, did you roll off that log *on purpose?*" Austin asked.

Abe's blue eyes grew sober. "You know I wouldn't do that," he said. "We'd get punished for swimming on Sunday."

"I know," Austin nodded uncomfortably. "We better promise not to tell."

Abe looked at his friend. "Promising isn't enough," Abe said. "We've got to *swear.* Put up your right hand."

"Swear by the Sun and Moon and Dog Star that we'll never tell a *soul*," Abe said. He was as solemn as a judge.

10

Austin shivered. "Oh, I swear," he said quickly.

Abe's friend kept his word. He never told the secret until many years later. He did not tell until after Abe Lincoln had grown up to be a great President and had been killed.

"Abe and I promised we wouldn't tell," Austin Gollaher said then. "When Abe Lincoln made a promise, *he kept it!*"

Chapter *2*

Firelight

"Who can spell Mississippi?" the teacher pointed his ruler at the class.

Abe Lincoln's long arm shot up. "M-i-s-s-i-s-s-i-p-p-i," he said, all in one breath.

Abe was bright in school. He was always the last one standing in a spell-down. But there were few school days for pioneer children. They had to work as hard as their fathers and mothers.

In good weather they were needed for chores in the fields, so they stayed home. On winter mornings it was sometimes too snowy for the children to walk to school. The prairie winds blew cold.

To help keep warm, each child held a hot potato. It had been roasted in the coal fire. The children held the potatoes in their mittened hands on the long walk. They ate the potatoes with their lunch. On the walk home, their fingers and toes were often frost-nipped.

Sometimes there were not enough families among the pioneer settlers to have a school. Other times there was no teacher in the lonely country.

Abe Lincoln had one sister, Nancy. She was two years older than Abe.

They went to school like other pioneer children—here and there, now and then.

But Abe learned to read. He read even at home, beginning with the Bible. Then he walked miles to find other books. He would knock on a farm-house door. "Please, have you any book I could borrow?" Abe would ask. "I'll be careful of it and be sure to bring it back."

Abe borrowed *Aesop's Fables, Pilgrim's Progress*, a life of George Washington and a farmer's *Almanac*. He read every word carefully, lying in front of the fire for light. He also learned to write and to do arithmetic. A charred stick was Abe's pencil. He spelled out words on the wooden fireshovel. He figured sums in arithmetic.

Abe Lincoln's father was a carpenter. Their furniture was homemade. There were tables and benches and a feather bed.

Families could be happy, even with few comforts. The Lincoln house was a happy one.

Like most pioneers, the Lincolns moved often. They would hear of a place where there was better land. Then they would load the family furniture into a wagon. They tied the cow behind the wagon and moved on to a new home.

Young Abe never minded moving. He knew his father would build another log cabin. There would be another creek to fish and new friends to meet. Abe was always quick to make friends.

Sometimes the new friends thought young Abe was lazy. He could chop a tree, or plough a field, or build a fence as fast as any boy. But they thought Abe spent too much time reading. They thought that made him different.

When Abe was ten years old, his family moved to Indiana. Later that year something happened that made Abe really different. His mother, pretty, gentle Nancy Hanks Lincoln, died.

Then life was very lonely for young Abe and his sister. There was no fire to come home to at night. There was only a cold, bare cabin with a dirt floor. Their mother's spinning wheel stood idle. There was no one to spin the yarn or weave cloth.

Abe's long arms and legs grew out of his jackets and trousers. His sister Nancy's skirts climbed above her knees. There was no one to make new clothes for the children or mend the old ones.

Chapter *3*

Footprints

One happy day Abe's father brought home a new wife, Sarah Bush Lincoln. Abe and Nancy liked their cheerful, kind stepmother. She brought three children of her own, John, Sarah and Matilda, to be a stepbrother and sisters to Abe and Nancy.

Now the house was lively again, with five children in it. Sarah Lincoln was a busy mother. She kept the house clean and a kettle of hot food cooking.

She listened to the children talk and laughed at their fun.

One day Abe played a joke. The ceiling had just been whitewashed. Dennis Hanks, Abe's older cousin, loved mischief as much as Abe did. Abe got Dennis to boost him upside down on his shoulders. Then Abe reached up and made footprints across the clean white ceiling. Abe was sure his stepmother would be puzzled. She would wonder who could have walked on the ceiling.

Abe's stepmother took one look at the footprints.

"Nobody but Abe Lincoln would ever have thought up such a thing," she said. Even though the ceiling was spoiled, she laughed. Abe cheerfully helped his stepmother clean up.

Later, he wrote in his copybook:

Abraham Lincoln, his hand and pen,

He will be good, but God knows when.

Life was busy for young Abe. His new mother helped him get over his loneliness. He was glad to be part of a family again.

Still Abe never forgot what it had felt like to be lonely and unhappy. All his life, it made him understand other people who were unhappy. Abe could remember the nights he had listened to the prairie wind blow sadly. He remembered wondering whether he would ever stop feeling lonesome.

When Abe grew older he worked harder. He helped his father farm. He milked cows and chopped down trees.

Some of the other farmers hired Abe to work for them.

Abe's favorite chore was taking grain to the mill. He had to wait for his turn to have the grain ground into flour. He had plenty of time to listen to the men talk and swap stories. Abe loved to swap stories.

No matter how much he worked, Abe always found time to read.

Abe's father was impatient. "The boy is wasting his time with books," he said.

Abe's mother had understood why Abe wanted to read. His stepmother understood too. "Let him read," she said. "Abe takes his time learning things. But he learns them right.

Someday he'll know everything in those books. Just wait and see."

All his life, Abe Lincoln remembered his own mother. He never forgot his stepmother's kindness and patience. When he had been elected President, he went back to visit his stepmother before he went to Washington.

Chapter *4*

Indian War

When Abe Lincoln was a young man he left his family and went to earn a living in New Salem, Illinois.

Abe had grown very tall. He was as lanky as ever, with broad shoulders and long legs. Abe seldom bothered to dress up much. But there was a nice look about Abe Lincoln, in spite of his careless clothes. His landlady said: "Abe doesn't always look exactly like a fine gentleman, but he acts like one."

New Salem was a little town. There were only a hundred people. Still it was more lively than living in a cabin on the lonely prairie. Abe liked having neighbors nearby. He was as quick as always to make friends.

Everybody liked Abe, though sometimes they felt he was a little different. In spite of his fun, he seemed serious. He thought about many things outside the little town. He wondered about the world, and life, and what was right and wrong.

Sometimes Abe's friends were puzzled. But they admired him. "Abe Lincoln is sure to be a success," they said. "But first he'll have to make up his mind what to be a success *at!*"

It was true that Abe had a hard time deciding what kind of work he wanted to do. He worked as a farmer and a carpenter. Then he worked in a sawmill and on the river boats. He also worked in politics now and then. Abe was always looking for other work to try.

When there was a war with the Indians, Abe stopped worrying about what job he should choose. He had to go with the other men to fight.

In pioneer days there were many fights between the Indians and the settlers. Both sides did unfair things in battle.

Chief Black Hawk was on the warpath. He burned down the settlers' houses and left many bloody scalps.

New Salem sent a volunteer company to fight the Indians. Abe Lincoln was in the company. There were no real officers. When the company voted for a captain they elected Abraham Lincoln.

Abe was pleased with the honor. He was glad the other men liked him.

One day an Indian came into Lincoln's camp. The Indian was helpless and unarmed. He had a safe-conduct pass. The pass meant the Indian could go through the battle line without being attacked or hurt.

Some of the men in Lincoln's company were restless. They felt homesick and mean. "We were sent to kill Indians," they said. "Here's an Indian. Let's kill him."

Captain Lincoln stopped them. "Let the Indian go," he ordered.

Abe Lincoln knew his men might be angry. They might not want him to be their captain any more. But he took the chance.

The Indian went free.

The men saw that Abe had been honest enough to take the chance of not being liked. They liked Abe all the more.

Abe Lincoln went on being captain.

Chapter *5*

The Barrel

When the Indian war was over, Abe went back to work. He kept a store. At the same time he was postmaster of New Salem. He worked as a surveyor also. A surveyor measures land for people.

Keeping store was the job that suited Abe best so far. There weren't many customers in the little town. When the store was empty, Abe had time to read his books.

In summer he read outdoors under a tree. When the weather was bad, he stretched his long legs on the store counter and went on reading.

Still Abe was not satisfied. He didn't want to be a storekeeper all his life. "If only I could find some work where reading books is important," Abe thought.

One day a farmer drove up to Lincoln's store. The farmer had his wife and children and his furniture packed on a wagon. "We're crowded," the farmer said to Abe Lincoln. "I've got to leave something behind. Will you take this barrel? Pay me half a dollar and you can keep it."

Abe gave the farmer half a dollar. When he unpacked the barrel, Abe found something that changed his whole life. At the bottom, under some old shoes, he found a thick book. It was a copy of *Blackstone's Commentaries*—the most important law book ever printed.

That night Abe Lincoln began to read *Blackstone*. Abe remembered a Major Stuart he had met in the Indian war. "If you ever want to be a lawyer," Major Stuart had told Abe, "come and see me. I need a partner."

A lawyer was a man who understood laws and helped people who were in trouble. A lawyer could help them tell their story in court. In court a judge decided what was right and fair. A lawyer could help a person be fairly treated.

Abe Lincoln had always liked to see people get what was fair. He decided to try to be a lawyer.

It took Abe many long months to study *Blackstone.* He wrote to Major Stuart that he had started to study law. Major Stuart sent him more books to read.

In those days, most young lawyers did not go to law school. They read and studied law by themselves and were helped by an older lawyer. Major Stuart helped Abe.

Abe went on working while he studied. His store failed and Abe had debts he could not pay. He was more determined than ever to be a lawyer. Then he could earn money and pay his debts.

At last the day came when Abe passed his examinations. Abraham Lincoln was a lawyer.

He went to Springfield, Illinois. Major Stuart kept his promise. He took Abe into his law office.

Mr. Stuart introduced his young partner to his family.

One of John Stuart's cousins was a young lady named Mary Todd. Mary had light brown curls and blue eyes. She had grown up in Kentucky. Now she lived with her married sister in Springfield. Mary Todd was very popular. She had lots of beaux who could bow politely and dance gracefully.

Abe Lincoln was too awkward to bow politely. His feet were too big to dance properly.

With a twinkle in her eye, Mary told her sister, "Mr. Lincoln said he wanted to dance with me in the worst way—and *he certainly did!*"

But Mary liked Abe Lincoln best of all the young men she knew.

Abraham Lincoln and Mary Todd were married in her sister's parlor.

Chapter *6*

Pig Under a Fence

Now Abe Lincoln was a lawyer and a married man. It was time to settle down.

The first Lincoln baby was a boy. He was named Robert Todd Lincoln for Mary's father. After Robert was born, the Lincolns bought a house.

Mary Lincoln was very busy at home. When little Eddie was born, there were two babies to take care of. Mary mended, baked and kept the house tidy.

She made her husband's white linen shirts herself.

Abe Lincoln worked hard in his law office. He took good care of his family. He paid back his debts from the store in New Salem. After that, Abe Lincoln was never in debt again.

Hard work did not make Abe Lincoln forget how to get along with people. He had as many friends as ever. He never forgot to be gentle.

Once, on his way to court, Abe Lincoln saw a man beating a horse. Abe dropped his law papers and ran to take the man's hand. When the man promised to stop whipping the poor horse, Abe Lincoln picked up his law papers and went on into the Court House.

Abe Lincoln never liked to see a person or an animal treated cruelly. Another day he was riding far out in the country. He saw a pig stuck under a fence. Abe Lincoln stopped his horse and got out of the buggy. He had to pry up a heavy fence to get the pig loose. Finally the pig ran free, squealing happily.

The lawyer who was riding with Abe Lincoln was impatient. "Why do you bother about a pig?" the lawyer asked.

Abe Lincoln shook his head. "I don't know," he said. "Only I don't like to see anything not *free!*"

Abe Lincoln still loved to tell stories.

Once a judge was angry because Lincoln was whispering to a friend in court.

The friend laughed out loud. The judge made Abe pay a fine of five dollars.

Afterward the judge asked Abe Lincoln, "What was that story you told?"

Abe told the story again. The judge laughed too. He gave Abe Lincoln back the five dollars.

Abe Lincoln was a good lawyer. He won many cases in court. He could speak well to defend his side.

People in Springfield began to say, "If you want a lawyer, get Abe Lincoln. He's smart—and he's honest!"

Lincoln's law office was a busy place. But Abe Lincoln spent plenty of time with his family. He loved to play with the children.

Little Eddie Lincoln had died. But, besides Robert, the Lincolns had two younger sons. Willie and Tad loved mischief as much as their father. They would wait for their father to walk home from his office. Other neighborhood children waited too. Abe Lincoln was very tall. When he wore his high, black, stove-pipe hat, the children could see him coming a block away. They would run to meet him with shouts. The first one to reach Abe got a ride home on his shoulders.

One morning Abe Lincoln walked past a neighbor's yard. He saw eight-year-old Josephine Remann standing at the gate. She wore her best coat and bonnet, but she was crying bitterly.

Abe Lincoln stopped. "Whatever is the matter, Josephine?" he asked.

Josephine sobbed harder. "I'm going on the steamcars to visit in Decatur. It's my first trip on the train alone. But the wagon didn't call for my trunk. It's too big for Mamma to carry. And my Papa isn't home. So *I can't go —*"

Abe Lincoln swung the trunk on his shoulder and took the little girl by the hand. "Come along, Josephine," he said. "I'll take your trunk to the station. I'm as good as a wagon any day."

Chapter 7

Torchlight

More and more people began to know Abraham Lincoln. They respected his work as a lawyer and as a speaker. Abe had always liked politics. Now he began to be important in politics too. He was elected to the United States Congress. He went to Washington.

When Abe Lincoln's term in Congress was finished, he came back to Springfield. He worked in his law office. He went on working in politics too.

He made many speeches. People who heard him, said, "Abe Lincoln will be a great man some day."

Abraham Lincoln had to decide about a very important question. It was the question of slavery.

Half of the states in America were saying, "Slavery is wrong. One person should not buy another person and own him."

The other states said, "We must decide what is right for ourselves. If we cannot, then we will leave the Union."

Abe Lincoln was a very fair man. He wanted everyone to have a fair chance. Years ago, Abe had been fair to the Indian when the men in his company started to kill him.

Abraham Lincoln thought a long time about the question of slavery.

Abe Lincoln made up his mind. "I must go against slavery," he said. He made an important speech. *"I do not believe a country can be half-slave and half-free,"* he said.

Abraham Lincoln believed all the states of the country must stay together. The Union must be saved. He made many more speeches. He argued with other men in politics.

Many people thought Lincoln's speeches were right. Many others thought he was wrong.

When Abe Lincoln came home from making a speech, Mrs. Lincoln and the boys hugged him.

"Whether I'm right or wrong," Abe said, "my family still seems glad to see me."

In 1860 enough people believed Abraham Lincoln was right to nominate him for President of the United States. His family and friends and neighbors all hoped he would be elected.

The weeks before the election were exciting. Important men came to call at the Lincoln house. There were judges and senators and governors. There were newspaper reporters.

Willie and Tad were used to seeing important men. They ran in and out of the parlor, no matter what dignified gentlemen were calling on their father.

When election day came, people all over the country voted for the next President.

The news came that Abraham Lincoln had been elected.

That night there was a torchlight parade in Springfield. Everyone in town marched to the Lincoln house, carrying lighted torches.

The oldest Lincoln boy, Robert, was away at college. But the little boys, Tad and Willie, stayed up long past their bedtime to watch the parade.

Mrs. Lincoln and her sisters worked to give all the visitors something to eat. They had to borrow more coffee and cookies from all the neighbors.

Willie and Tad sat on the gate-posts of the Lincoln house. "Do you want to see Old Abe?" they asked the visitors. "Give us a nickel, and we'll show him to you."

Chapter 8

The White House

When it was time to leave for Washington, Willie and Tad were sad. It was exciting to have their father elected President. But the boys did not want to leave home.

The boys begged to take their dog, Fido, with them. Fido belonged half to Willie and Tad and half to the Roll boys, who were their best friends.

"How can we take half of Fido to Washington?" Abe Lincoln asked.

"We don't know which half of Fido is ours!" To comfort the boys, he promised they could have a pony in Washington.

The Lincolns moved to the White House in 1861.

Abraham Lincoln was President of the United States.

Mr. Lincoln's family soon found out that the President had to work hard all day long. There were always crowds of people at his office door. Mr. Lincoln tried to see them all. He thought everyone had a right to talk to the President.

It was often late at night before Mr. Lincoln could leave his office. But busy as he was, he kept his promise to Willie and Tad. He got them a pony.

Even with a pony to play with, the boys were restless.

They were very lonely for their friends back home. Their mother was lonely too. Many times they all wanted to be back in Springfield, where Mr. Lincoln had more time to be with his family.

When the Civil War began the President was even busier. He still played with the boys when he could or took Mrs. Lincoln for a drive. But night after night, the light burned in the President's office. He talked with the generals of the Northern Army. Abraham Lincoln had to make many decisions alone.

"The North believes slavery is wrong," Mr. Lincoln said. "The Southern states want to break away and govern themselves. The people on both sides believe they are right. The soldiers on both sides are fighting bravely."

He walked back and forth, back and forth in his office, waiting for the terrible news of battle losses.

One day Willie and Tad wanted to see their father. They waited impatiently outside his office. When the door was opened the boys slipped in. They played around their father's desk all morning. The President went on with his work. He wasn't disturbed by the boys playing.

Later the President had a cabinet meeting. The most important men in the country sat at the table. Tad and Willie hid under the table and played around the men's feet. The important men were angry. They didn't think children should be allowed to disturb older people.

Mr. Lincoln's secretary offered to shut the boys out of the room.

"No," Mr. Lincoln said. "All over the country boys are dying. Let the boys have fun when they can. Don't shut them out."

Chapter *9*

Gettysburg

The battle of Gettysburg was one of the worst battles of the war. It went on for several days. Mr. Lincoln waited up late for the reports.

A long time after Tad had fallen asleep, Mrs. Lincoln came down to the President's office. "Come and rest," she begged her husband. "You can't help the poor boys who are fighting."

"No," Mr. Lincoln shook his head sadly.

"At least I can stay awake thinking about them. Our best young men are dying in both the North and the South."

Abraham Lincoln never felt that the southern people were enemies. He believed that *war* was the enemy.

After the battle of Gettysburg, Mr. Lincoln went to dedicate a cemetery there. His heart was heavy. "How can I make a speech?" he asked Mrs. Lincoln. "No words are as important as what the soldiers did at Gettysburg."

On the train going to Gettysburg, Mr. Lincoln wrote down a few lines for his speech.

The next day the President read these lines:

"Fourscore and seven years ago, our fathers brought forth on this continent a new nation, conceived in liberty and dedicated to the proposition that all men are created equal . ."

The President's speech ended with the beautiful words:

". . . that government of the people, by the people, for the people, shall not perish from the earth."

Today, almost a hundred years later, Abraham Lincoln's speech at Gettysburg is known all over the world.

One winter during the war, Willie Lincoln was very sick. His fever got worse. The President and Mrs. Lincoln left an important party at the White House. They sat by Willie's bed.

Willie asked to see his pony. The President had the pony led under the window. That cheered the sick boy a little.

But Willie died.

It was the saddest loss Abraham Lincoln and his wife ever felt. Tad missed his brother. He and Willie had always played together.

"All over the country families have lost their sons," Mr. Lincoln said. "Now we have lost ours. We must try to be as brave as the other families have been."

When spring came, Robert Lincoln came home from college on vacation. The Lincolns were glad to see him. They tried to be cheerful for Robert's sake.

Mr. Lincoln read that two nanny-goats were for sale. "They'll make fine new pets for Tad," he said. He bought them so his son would not be so lonely.

The whole family laughed to see the saucy goats, harnessed to a little red wagon. Tad drove them. He raced the goats up and down the White House driveway. They nearly upset General Grant when he came to call on the President. Sometimes Tad took the goats into the White House with him.

Later when Tad and his mother were away on a trip, Mr. Lincoln found one of the goats sleeping on Tad's bed. The goat had chewed the spread. Mr. Lincoln chased the goat back to the barn. When the busy President sent a telegram to Mrs. Lincoln, he took time to add: *"Tell Tad the goats are well."*

Chapter 10

Sunset

The Civil War lasted four years. It ended in 1865. President Lincoln signed the order that made the slaves in the South free. Soon there would be no more slavery in America.

All the states were united again. The Union was saved. But the damages of war had to be mended. The country must be led back to peace.

Abraham Lincoln was elected President for a second term.

"The hardest work is over," Mr. Lincoln told his wife. "Now we can be a family again." He smiled. But he looked old. His face was lined with worry.

One evening Mrs. Lincoln wanted to cheer up the President. She asked him to take her to the theater.

The President and Mrs. Lincoln sat in a box. Halfway through the play a shot was fired. President Lincoln was killed.

An actor named John Wilkes Booth had shot the President. Booth was a weird, half crazy person, who had been upset by the war.

People all over the country, North and South, were shocked by the terrible news.

Now Mrs. Lincoln had lost her husband. Robert and Tad had lost their father. The whole country had lost its great leader, Abraham Lincoln.

The train that carried President Lincoln back home to Springfield was draped in black. Crowds of people stood by the railroad tracks in every city and town. Some waited all night on lonesome country roads to see the train go by. Many of the people wept.

The train moved slowly. Its mournful whistle blew across the prairie where young Abe Lincoln had lived.

Abraham Lincoln was buried in Springfield, Illinois, where he lived the happiest years with his family. His house where they lived still stands there.

The rooms are just as the Lincolns left them.

In Washington, D.C., the Lincoln Memorial makes Americans remember their great President. There is a beautiful statue of Lincoln. His face looks down on the thousands of people who come there. It makes each one feel the deep kindness and understanding that Abraham Lincoln showed to all people while he lived.

Other books by Anne Colver